mandy moore

THE UNOFFICIAL · BOOK ·

mandy moore

THE UNOFFICIAL BOOK

Molly MacDermot

BILLBOARD
BOOKS

Created in 2000 by
Virgin Books
An imprint of
Virgin Publishing Ltd
Thames Wharf Studios
Rainville Road
London
W6 9HA

First published in the United States in 2000 by Billboard Books, an
imprint of Watson-Guptill Publications, a division of BPI
Communications Inc., at 770 Broadway, New York, NY 10003

ISBN 0 8230 8374 8

Printed and bound in the United Kingdom by Butler and Tanner
Ltd, Frome and London

Colour Origination by Colourwise Ltd

Designed by DW Design, London. www.dwdesign.co.uk
First printing 2000

1 2 3 4 5 6 7 8 9/06 05 04 03 02 01 00

PICTURE CREDITS
Alpha
Jeff Spicer 29, 35, 51, 61

Caught In The Act
Scott Harrison 48

Corbis
Everett 36, 48

Globe Photos
Fitzroy Barrett 20, 25, 58, 59
Lisa O'Connor 47

Retna
Bill Davila 18, 23, 49
Kelly A. Swift 34, 37
Barry Talesnick 33, 42, 43, 45

South Beach
Joe Marone 31, 32, 40, 53, 57

Star File
Alex Lloyd Gross 8, 10, 13, 26, 27
Todd Kaplan 2, 4, 7, 15, 17, 19, 22,
28, 38, 39, 44, 50, 52, 55, 56, 62
Jeffrey Mayer 41
VDL 9, 21, 46

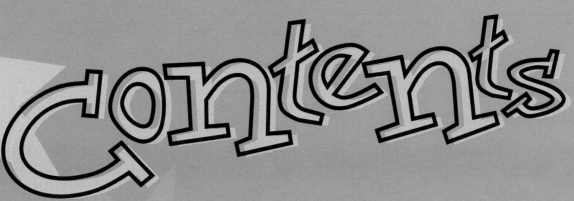

Contents

Chapter One

Sweet as Candy

IT'S NOT SURPRISING MANDY MOORE'S FIRST SINGLE WAS called "Candy" – it's a sweet song from an even sweeter star. While some pop princesses can let fame spoil them, Mandy remains naturally warm and friendly, dispelling the myth that fame turns you into a demanding diva. In fact, her pleasant personality permeates everything she puts her energies into, whether she's singing on stage, promoting Neutrogena or hosting her own show for MTV. Mandy has a special talent for lighting up a room with just a simple flash of her smile. It's that friendly vibe which fans find refreshing, and that's why Mandy has turned into an amazing multi-genre performer who is making musical waves across the world from New York to London and Hong Kong.

Mandy was just six years old when she discovered that performing was her dream. It was 1990 in Orlando, Florida, and the blonde first-grader with the big smile was watching a school production of the musical *Oklahoma*. Mandy remembers sitting in the audience feeling "mesmerized" and realizing that she too wanted to be singing and dancing on stage. Little did she know that her dream would come true faster than she had ever imagined.

Fast forward nine years to the summer of 1999: Mandy is fifteen and fulfilling her dream of being on stage, only she's not in a school, she's singing in a sold-out stadium as the opening act for one of the hottest groups on the planet – 'N Sync. Following that tour, Mandy sealed her success by releasing her first single "Candy" on August 17, 1999. The catchy love tune went Gold and its eyecatching video became a regular on MTV's *Total Request Live*.

Later that year Mandy landed a spot on the Backstreet Boys tour, and on December 7, 1999 she released her debut album *So Real*, which was so successful it went Platinum. *So Real* soon made Mandy's life "surreal", because suddenly everyone wanted to know about this new girl from the Sunshine State. Mandy was heading towards the dizzying heights of stardom, and it was happening so quickly she has said it felt like one big blur. Her website, www.mandymoore.com, was reportedly receiving 100,000 hits a day.

Recently there has been a new wave of blonde female teen solo artists just like Mandy Moore, giving the male artists a run for their money. These include Britney Spears, Christina Aguilera, Jessica Simpson and Hoku. Much of the late 1990s was dominated by guy groups and male solo artists who dominated MTV with their muscles and testosterone, but the current explosion of girl power in the new millennium proves there's plenty of room in the music world for everyone.

With the proliferation of pop princesses taking audiences by storm, there are bound to be comparisons. While Mandy would agree there are some similarities between herself and other female solo artists, she thinks it's naive for critics to lump the girls together just because they may have similar hair and sing about love. To the well-trained ears and eyes of loyal fans, there is little difficulty setting Mandy apart from the rest.

For starters, Mandy is younger than most of her pop peers. She turned sweet sixteen on April 10, 2000, so being the baby of the bunch meant she wasn't old enough to join Britney Spears and Christina Aguilera on Disney's variety show *The New Mickey Mouse Club* in the early 1990s. It just goes to show you can still be a pop star today without having *MMC* on your resumé!

She wants to be known as a singer who can dance rather than a dancer who can sing – although she's impressing fans with **her talent** for both.

Instead, Mandy perfected her performing skills by joining local acting groups, ballet and vocal classes. Another difference is that Mandy is taller than the others; she stands almost six feet tall in platforms, and she's still growing.

More importantly, Mandy's signature style exudes a sweetness and appeal exclusive to her. Music industry supporters often remark on her warm voice, which can be heard in the uplifting hit "I Wanna Be With You" on her new album of the same name. Mandy has described her music as pop with an edge – her uptempo dance tunes glimmer with hints of rock and her ballads are bolstered with R&B. She wants to be known as a singer who can dance rather than a dancer who can sing – although she's impressing fans with her talent for both. Mandy's songs are about subjects that affect her – boys, love, and relationships – and which ring true for girls universally.

Mandy truly marks her individuality with the attitude "it's cool to be a teen" – she shuns super-sexy outfits

and has said she doesn't feel the need to act and dress like she's twenty to be successful. Mandy is having too much fun being sixteen, which means shopping for cute outfits at stores like Guess and Abercrombie & Fitch, chatting with her friends on the phone, and dreaming about heartthrobs like actor Ryan Phillippe. Mandy is showing her fans that you can be sweet, humble and down-to-earth even in the face of fame, and that if you have a dream you can make it come true regardless of your age.

Ten Things We Love About Mandy

1 Mandy is proud of her big feet: Mandy's model height explains her big feet – she wears a size 10 shoe. She has recalled her embarrassment when boys come up to her and compare their shoe size with hers. They call her "bigfoot," but she doesn't care. She thinks they're cool feet.

2 She's a girlie-girl: She loves pink and she can't leave home without her lip gloss. She is especially fond of cotton candy and strawberry-flavored gloss.

3 She's natural: Mandy doesn't believe in changing herself and has said she would never get plastic surgery. She can't understand why people would want to mess with nature and alter their natural features just to make someone else happy or to grab attention.

4 She loves animals: Mandy has three cats – Milo, Chloe and Zoe – who receive special attention when Mandy is home with them in Orlando. She has said that she misses her cat trio terribly when she's on tour. She would like to add more additions to her pet family when she finds the time and says she's looking for a puppy, specifically a Teacup Yorkshire Terrier.

5 **She has a sweet tooth**: Mandy's aptly named song "Candy" says it all. This girl has a weakness for all that is sugar-coated, including cotton candy, Snickers chocolate bars and Jolly Ranchers. When she's touring, she searches each venue for people selling cotton candy. She has said she limits her intake to two or three helpings of the pink stuff a week while she's on tour. For Christmas, Mandy received a cotton candy machine so she can now make the treat herself.

6 **She takes care of herself**. Mandy may be a sucker for sweet treats, but she also knows the importance of keeping healthy so she's always fit for her fans. She drinks plenty of water for clear skin, she tries to get eight hours of sleep nightly, and she eats her vegetables – especially carrots – to make her eyes sparkle.

7 **She's a homebody**: When she gets the time off, Mandy loves lounging at home with her mother, father, and two brothers. She is also very close to her grandmother, who was a dancer on the London stage.

8 **She cherishes her friends**: Mandy has said that she runs up big phone bills because she insists on keeping in touch with her friends even when she's touring. She also e-mails them when she can, invites them to appear in her videos, and brings them to movie premieres. She's never too busy for her best buds.

9 **She's not scared**: Mandy is a gutsy girl who can handle wild rollercoaster rides. In fact, her fave Disney World ride is the twenty-minute thriller "Alien Encounter." She also took the dare and went parasailing in the Florida Keys. This girl is definitely not faint-hearted!

10 **She helps others**: Mandy sang on a charity album called "Give the Kids The World," and fans can see the pre-record deal Mandy acting in a new home video, "Magic Al and The Mind Factory," which helps children get over their fear of the dark. Mandy also supports and performs with fellow Orlando singer Kimberly Thach, who is a Leukemia survivor and the National Youth Ambassador for the Leukemia and Lymphoma Society. The two friends met through the Make-a-Wish Foundation.

Mandy loves...

Actress: Gwyneth Paltrow

Actor: Ryan Phillippe

Music: Lauryn Hill, Macy Gray, Missy Elliott, Shania Twain, Enrique Iglesias and Top 40 radio

She grew up listening to: Madonna, Janet Jackson, New Kids On The Block and The Spice Girls

Singers: Madonna, Karen Carpenter, Natalie Imbruglia

Role model: Bette Midler

Movie: *Beaches*

Morning food: Bagels

Sweet treat: Cotton Candy

Fast food restaurant: Wendy's

Food: Sushi

Sport: Lacrosse

Decade: She thinks the 1970s would have been fun

Television show: *7th Heaven*, MTV's *Total Request Live*, *The Tom Green Show*

Cartoon: MTV's *Daria*

School subjects: English and French

Book: *A Land Remembered* by Patrick D. Smith

Ice cream: Peanut butter cup

Animal: Monkey

Song on *So Real*: "Walk Me Home"

Hobby: Shopping, surfing the web

Places to visit: New Zealand, Australia and Japan

City: New York City

The Essentials

Date of birth: April 10, 1984
Born: Nashua, New Hampshire
Home town: Orlando, Florida
Sign: Aries
Eyes: Hazel
Worst habit: Biting her nails
Scared of: Butterflies
Siblings: She has an older brother, Scott, and a younger brother, Kyle
Special talent: She's double-jointed
Biggest fear: Losing someone she loves

Chapter Two

Mandy's First Love

ONE OF THE MOST MAGICAL MOMENTS IN LIFE IS discovering your first love. For some, that first love may be the cute boy next door, an inspiring ballet class or anything else that puts a bounce in your step. For Mandy, performing was her first love and that memorable trip to see *Oklahoma* when she was in first grade was only the beginning. From that moment on, Mandy found singing and dancing an inspiration – it gave her that unmistakable rush – and she was determined to make performing her life no matter how hard she needed to work.

Amanda Leigh Moore was born on April 10, 1984 in Nashua, New Hampshire, a former mill town which was once named the best place in the US to live by *Money* magazine. Her parents Don, an American Airlines pilot, and Stacy, who worked as a journalist, already had a first-born son, Scott, so they were thrilled to have a daughter join the family. Six weeks after Mandy was born, the family decided to pack their bags and head south to Orlando, Florida, a city of over a million people. There the Moores' world took on a new look – suddenly they were surrounded by sunshine, amusement parks and entertainment complexes. Orlando is the home of Disney World, Nickelodeon and several TV production companies, partly because the reliability of the warm weather makes outdoor filming practical. A couple of years after moving to Orlando, Mandy's parents had another son, Kyle, who appears in Mandy's "Candy" video.

It was a good thing Mandy's parents decided to move to Orlando when she was just six weeks old, because it allowed her to grow up in a town that has

fostered a roster of stars including 'N Sync, Backstreet Boys, Britney Spears and Christina Aguilera. Orlando, or O-Town as it is nicknamed, is also the location for Trans Continental Studios, the hit factory founded by Louis Pearlman, who once managed Backstreet Boys and 'N Sync.

Growing up, Mandy was a girlie-girl who liked to play with her Barbie dolls and wear pretty dresses. Her mother Stacy had a rule for Mandy: she could only wear a dress to school if it was at least 70°F (21°C) outside. Every morning, Stacy would call the weather to check on the temperature. Mandy remembers whining and crying if it was too cold outside, but since the Moores lived in sunny Florida, the odds were good for Mandy.

Mandy has said that one of her first musical memories is jumping up and down on her bed belting out Madonna's 1986 hit "Papa Don't Preach." Although at age six she was too young to understand the meaning of the song, Mandy knew she was crazy about the catchy melody. She has said that Madonna is one of her great influences because she doesn't limit herself and she's constantly experimenting with new looks and different musical styles. Mandy grew up listening to her earlier albums like *True Blue*, and continues to listen today to the pop legend who has influenced so many of today's new artists.

In third grade, Mandy mustered the nerve to audition for a part in the school play and

before long she was starring in musicals like *Guys and Dolls*, *South Pacific* and *Bye Bye Birdie*. Mandy learned a lot from each show and realized that it takes a lot of discipline, devotion and determination to be a performer. Plus, she had to learn how to squeeze in homework. Mandy has said that she always liked school and admits she probably sounds weird for saying so.

For two summers, the ever-energetic Mandy enrolled at Stagedoor Manor Academy, a prestigious performing arts school in Loch Sheldrake, New York, where she practised what she loved most – the art of performing. She missed her friends terribly and kept in touch by writing them long letters, but she knew she would be bored if she wasn't pursuing her dreams.

By the time she was ten, Mandy had convinced her parents that her passion for performing was not a passing fancy but a serious ambition, and that she truly wanted to improve her musical skills by taking singing lessons. Don and Stacy have said that their little songbird-in-training had begged them for at least four years after seeing her first musical before they finally relented and looked for a respected vocal coach to train their daughter.

Unlike traditional stage parents who plan their kids' careers while they're in the crib, Don and Stacy wanted Mandy to follow her own ambition without their pushing. Mandy remembers her mother meeting the vocal coach and asking her to be truthful about her daughter's potential as a singer. Stacy didn't want her daughter wasting her time and the teacher's time if there wasn't any talent to begin with. Well, there was little risk that anyone's time would be wasted because Mandy thoroughly impressed the vocal coach and immediately started lessons. It was important for Mandy to learn how to sing properly; she was taught how to breathe and sing from the diaphragm instead of the throat for a richer, stronger voice.

The New Mickey Mouse Club was cancelled in 1994 when Mandy was only ten, so she didn't have the chance to audition for the show like her showbiz peers. But Mandy was too busy anyway, taking singing and dance lessons, modelling, starring in commercials and performing on stage. She joined Civic Kids, a singing troupe affiliated with Civic Theatre of Central Florida, and dived into whatever project presented itself.

Mandy was still active in school, playing lacrosse and scoring straight As in

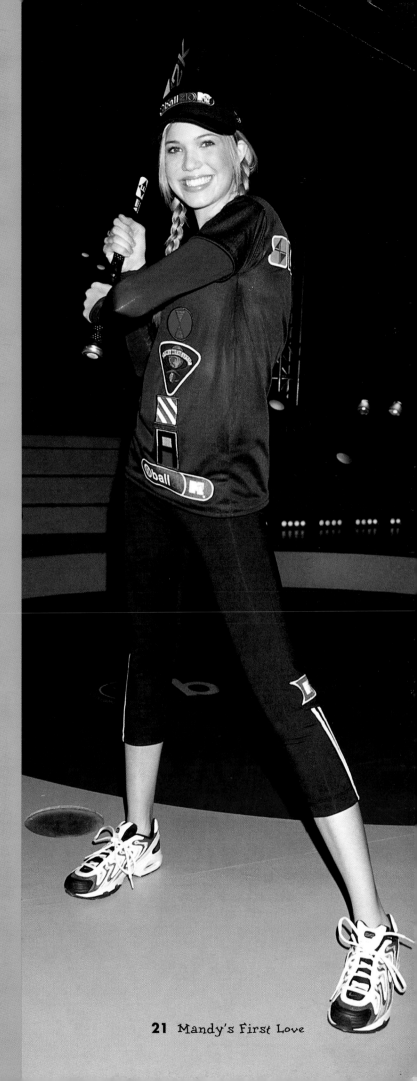

class, and has said her fave subjects were English and French, although she'd have preferred not to take Mathematics. Mandy is a self-described perfectionist who cares about her studies. She is also a perfectionist about her handwriting and writes neatly in block letters; when she's typing an e-mail she usually uses all upper case letters. Mandy tried cheerleading and basketball – thinking her height would be an advantage – only to discover she prefers watching sports. However, her prime focus was music. She credits performing for building her self-confidence, which came in handy during her junior high school days.

Mandy enjoyed starring in school plays but she was restless to branch out, so when she was twelve she sent a tape of herself singing "The Star-Spangled Banner" to the Orlando Magic basketball team. They were pleased with her pipes and asked Mandy to sing the National Anthem at their games. There was a domino effect and before long

Mandy was in demand to perform in front of thousands of people for other sports teams, including the Orlando Predators football team. She belted out the patriotic song over 100 times and was soon nicknamed the "National Anthem Girl." At thirteen, she had the chance to perform at the White House and was asked to sing a Christmas solo. Although she didn't get a glimpse of President Bill Clinton, she did see Socks, the resident cat.

Mandy started cutting jingles for commercials, recording voice-overs, working on television pilots and even provided the voice of Ducky for Universal Studios' "Land Before Time" attraction. She found herself spending more time in the recording studio than at the mall with her friends. She was landing one professional project after another and was cast in a kids' cartoon show about sea turtles and asked to sing the theme song. Although the pilot never aired on television, Mandy's work in the studio was not in vain because she was spotted by a couple of influential producers who liked her vocal range and style and suggested that she record a demo tape.

> Unlike other **pop artists** who dream of being on MTV, Mandy had originally envisioned herself as a **Broadway singer** and not a **recording artist**

Luck was on Mandy's side, because while she was in the studio she was overheard by a Federal Express delivery man, who also happened to be a part-time talent scout. He was so impressed with her polished sound that he sent Mandy's half-finished demo tape to his friend, Dave McPherson, who happened to be a big shot record producer at Sony. McPherson is the musical mastermind who signed Backstreet Boys when he worked at Jive records, and later became a senior vice-president at Epic Records, which is part of Sony. In December 1998 McPherson flew down to Florida to hear this budding star with his own ears, and discovered she was just the person Sony's Epic/550 label needed. Her warm sound, bubbly personality and good looks convinced him that she would appeal to a mass audience, and before she could say "I want a record deal" she had landed one that very weekend! McPherson would end up being the executive producer on her album and a guiding force in her career. He has called Mandy "magnetic" and "charismatic."

Mandy has said that her initial reaction to getting a record contract was shock; she thought she was too young and that the record company would wait until she was seventeen or eighteen before signing her. Unlike other pop artists who dream of being on MTV, Mandy had originally envisioned herself as a Broadway singer and not a recording artist, although she was ecstatic with her new found pop princess status.

Success Is So Real

Chapter Three

THE MOST IMPORTANT STEP IN GAINING A RECORD company's support is to wow not only the person who initially sought you out, but the whole group of executives who listen carefully to your every note during the audition. This high-powered presentation is not an easy task, but one Mandy tackled with the grace of a true professional.

When Mandy met with the rest of the team at Sony's Epic offices, she wowed them by performing a Broadway show tune. Most auditioning teens choose to sing a pop tune; Christina Aguilera sang Whitney Houston's "Run to Me" and Britney Spears sang Whitney's "I Have Nothing" for their big auditions. The hard-to-please executives were knocked out by Mandy's exceptional performance and poise and impressed with the young girl's maturity.

In the spring of 1999, Mandy buckled down and started spending 8 to 14 hours a day working on recording her debut album *So Real* at Trans Continental Studios where Backstreet Boys and 'N Sync had once worked on their own albums. She worked closely with producers Shaun Fisher and Tony Battaglia – who made the first demo tape for Backstreet Boys – and discovered how much work is required to put out an album. What many don't know is that her record label sent back the first demo of "Candy" to be reworked, but after the song's tempo and key was changed countless times in the studio, the producer finally let Mandy sing the song the way she had wanted to, and that became the final version that fans know and love today.

Mandy has spent a lot of time in recording studios working with expert producers and sound technicians, and has said that she's amazed how many

people are involved in making an album flawless. She admires the technical masterminds who mix, master and produce the songs, and true to Mandy's humble spirit she thinks she has the easy part as a singer.

When "Candy" was released on August 17, 1999, the response was tremendous. It flew up the charts and peaked at number eight on the *Billboard Hot 100 Singles Chart.* Soon girls everywhere were using the song's metaphor to describe their crush as "sweet as candy." The single was certified Gold by the Recording Industry Association of America (RIAA), it reached the Top Ten on SoundScan's Top Single Sales chart and it raced to the Top 15 on Radio Disney. The single was snatched off record store shelves at a rapid rate and her growing fanbase got to work dedicating websites to their new fave artist. Suddenly, Mandy's world was changing and the rising star was feeling overwhelmed that people were actually buying her music. She had never guessed her dream would become reality, and to this day she admits she is still in constant amazement.

Mandy will never forget the day MTV's *Total*

Suddenly, **Mandy's world** was changing and *the* **rising star** was feeling overwhelmed *that* people were **actually buying** *her music*

Request Live debuted her video for "Candy." She cried tears of happiness because her dreams had come true. Mandy's hard work during the years leading up to that one day had paid off – "Candy" was one of the most requested videos on the influential *TRL*.

Mandy's infectious personality is so appealing it won the hearts of executives at MTV, who immediately snatched Mandy up and placed her alongside Carson Daly, who hosts *Total Request Live*. The viewers liked her guest hosting so much that MTV let Mandy judge *Say What? Karaoke*, host several makeover specials, and more. Now she has a three year contract with MTV and is hosting her own daily show about fashion, beauty and current teen issues.

In the "Candy" video, Mandy can be seen driving a new green Volkswagen Beetle, but what many fans don't know is that Mandy was only fifteen during the filming of the video and couldn't drive, so a camera truck towed the car to make it look like she was driving. Mandy also had the chance to hang out with the cool, cute skateboarders featured in the video, who would crash into each other on their boards just for fun during breaks. She has said that when she's working on her videos she's always amazed at the number of people – adults no less – who are working so hard for the success of her song.

A day after shooting the "Candy" video, Mandy wasted little time and started the highly anticipated 'N Sync summer tour. When her hit-filled album *So Real* hit record stores on December 7, 1999, it was certified Platinum in just three months. Album reviewers have remarked on the way her "relaxed" attitude comes across on the CD, and have said that it sounds like she's having a great time. On April 18th 2000, the soundtrack for the motion picture *Center Stage* arrived in stores, featuring Mandy's song "I Wanna Be With You." The movie, which has been called a *Fame* for the new millennium, follows a group of young dancers trying to make it big in the highly competitive professional dance world. The video for "I Wanna Be With You" was directed by the talented English director Nigel Dick, who also directed videos for Britney Spears and Backstreet Boys. It showcases ballet dancing – not a subject that is often featured in pop videos. Viewers watch Mandy serenade famed dancer Sascha Radetsky, who plays the male lead in *Center Stage*, in a cathedral-like space that is actually an old hotel in Los Angeles. Mandy had to perform one scene over and over again to get the video absolutely perfect, which meant she heard her song over 100 times. She has said that she wouldn't have it any other way, because she knew all eyes would be watching every detail closely.

On May 9 Epic/550 decided to release a limited edition album, *I Wanna Be With You*, featuring the single of the same name along with a remix of "Candy" and several other new songs. Releasing two albums within six months is unheard of, but Mandy is proving that rules are there to be broken.

> Mandy has said that when she's working on her videos she's **always amazed** at the number of people – **adults no less** – who are working so hard for the success of her song.

Mandy on UK TV with TV presenter Gaby Roslin and pop star Billie Piper.

Touring With The Guys

Chapter Four

MANDY HAS HAD A LOT OF EXPERIENCE PERFORMING BEFORE A HUGE audience, but she'll never forget the first time she opened on 'N Sync's 1999 summer tour. She had succeeded in snagging a spot on one of the most coveted tours that year, and with such incredible exposure Mandy mania was about to unfold. She remembers opening for the guys at the Jones Beach Amphitheatre in Long Island, New York, on Friday July 16th, 1999, to an audience of over 20,000 screaming fans. The show started at 7.30pm on a typically hot, muggy New York night. She has said that the experience was "awesome" and, like other fans, she was speechless when she first met the popular group. Mandy remembers gasping every time Justin Timberlake walked by. After getting to know them, she realized they're just cool, down-to-earth guys who manage to keep their fame in check. During the tour, Mandy suddenly started receiving calls from people she hadn't heard from in a while – because they wanted 'N Sync's autographs! She can understand the fan frenzy because she's a fan of 'N Sync herself. Her fave song? "God Must Have Spent A Little More Time On You."

While it can be intimidating to be a female performer singing before a crowd of 30,000 people – most of whom are cheering for the guys – Mandy was just happy to be up there singing, dancing and living the dream. The audience picked up on her confidence and before long fans were waiting for up to two-and-a-half hours to get her autograph. What audiences love about Mandy is that she can warm up a crowd – or even a packed arena filled with tens of thousands of screaming fans – with her infectious stage presence. Mandy finds

performing rewarding because she gets to connect with her fans; she loves to see them singing the words and getting transported by the music. She has said that when she's up on stage performing, she instantly forgets about anything that is troubling her and lets the music soothe her. One point that Mandy likes to make clear is that she doesn't believe in lip-synching, because she knows fans want the live experience.

After the 'N Sync summer tour, Mandy joined the Backstreet Boys 1999 tour for a series of performances in the round, which means the audience encircles the performers. It makes for a much more personal atmosphere because you're closer to your fans than in an outdoor arena. Mandy prefers performing in a close setting, although it can be awkward during an embarrassing moment.

Mandy remembers one especially red-in-the-face humiliation during her very first show with Backstreet Boys in Philadelphia. The sound engineers had forgotten to turn on her ear monitors, so she couldn't hear anything that was going on. Being the true professional that she is, Mandy rolled with the punches and was able to get back on track and deliver the song without missing a beat.

Mandy will never forget that tour with Backstreet Boys and has said that she respects the guys for staying levelheaded in the light of their enormous fame. After her performance, she remembers the guys would be right there cheering her on and asking if she needed anything. They made her really feel like a part of the tour and she was so happy to be there. Mandy maintains a love for live performance and recently performed with one of her fave singers, Macy Gray, in front of

She has said that when she's up on stage performing, she instantly forgets about anything that is troubling her and lets the music soothe her.

an enthusiastic crowd. In the summer of 2000, Mandy will be working hard performing at radio-sponsored shows all around the country, meeting more of her fans up close.

So what would life be like if you jumped on the tour bus with Mandy? You would wake up early in either a hotel room or on the tour bus and eat breakfast. Then you would let Mandy complete several chapters of schoolwork, which she does through the Texas Tech University Extended Studies Program. If she has questions or problems with a subject, like mathematics, she e-mails her tutor for help. Even though Mandy admits it's hard to study on the road – she's surrounded by older people who are finished with school – she has achieved excellent grades and will probably graduate from high school early.

After studying, Mandy is often interviewed by magazines and newspapers. She has said that she'll sometimes have ten interviews back to back, which means talking non-stop for eight hours with only a brief break for lunch. By the time afternoon rolls around, Mandy goes to the venue to do a sound check and get ready for the upcoming show. When she was touring with 'N Sync, she had the chance to catch up with the guys over dinner before getting ready for the big performance.

One of her pre-concert rituals is to join hands with her four dancers – Dominic, Marcel, Jimmy and Kevin – and pray. To soothe her throat before a performance, Mandy has a cup of hot water with a twist of

Mandy will never forget that tour with **Backstreet Boys** and has said that she respects the guys for staying levelheaded in the light of their enormous fame.

orange. After her show, Mandy signs autographs and meets her new fans – she has said she will never get used to the feeling of someone wanting her autograph. After that, Mandy gets to enjoy the other acts, and when it's all done she jumps back on the tour bus for an overnight drive to the next city. To pass the time during long trips, Mandy watches movies with her dancers, plays cards and sleeps. Does that sound like a tough day or what?

If there's one performer who truly places her fans high on her priority list, it's Mandy. During an internet chat a fan asked Mandy what she would do if she

were to lose her voice right before a concert. Mandy said she would go out and have someone explain that she couldn't perform, but that she would refund everyone's money. Mandy loves her fans because they've allowed her to live her dreams – and that's something she will always be thankful for.

Mandy travels with the stuffed animals fans give her at performances, and if she has too many she donates them to children's hospitals. She surfs the web to check out the dozens of websites fans have dedicated to her and she writes a journal on her own website so fans can follow her tour. For MTV's *FANatic* series, Mandy was interviewed by a girl in college, which proves this rising star has fans of all ages.

Mandy's Beauty Secrets

Chapter Five

MANDY ISN'T A HIGH-maintenance diva who obsesses over her hair and makeup, but she does like to look good when she's performing or attending an awards show. While many performers are fawned over by stylists holding big cans of hairspray and scary fake eyelashes, Mandy prefers to do her own primping with barely-there make-up and simple hair styles. Her motto: Less is Moore.

Mandy's record company had originally planned to promote an older image for their new pop princess, but Mandy preferred being true to herself and sticking to a look she was comfortable with. She didn't want big hair and outlandish clothes, so she told the marketing people she wanted a simple and natural image. Neutrogena spotted Mandy's natural beauty and offered her a three-year worldwide contract to be their spokesgirl. Now she's

popping up in magazine ads and television commercials pitching their latest pimple remedy.

When it comes to hair, Mandy likes to experiment with her blonde locks, and opts for looks the girls in the audience can try at home. During a performance she prefers having her hair off her face, so she pulls back sections of hair into mini-knots. To snag this style, part your hair in four sections and add gel. Then twist each section tightly, wrap the hair around so it forms a baby bun on top of your head, and secure with a rubber band. Massive manes are all the rage, so Mandy has been experimenting with hair extensions to get that extra length. Mandy's extensions are made of human hair from Italy and every two to three months she sits for up to six hours to have them replaced. Mandy is a girl who likes to change, so she recently shortened her hair and likes to wear it in a Charlie's Angels-inspired style which includes a "flip" and "wings" – like Farrah Fawcett in the 1970's.

Mandy has enjoyed beauty makeovers ever since she was a kid and decided to give her Barbie dolls new haircuts. She chopped off their long curls and gave the dolls mohawks! Although she no longer goes for such extreme hair looks, she's been gaining lots of makeover experience by co-hosting MTV's "Mandy's Mountain Makeover" with R&B sensation Tyrese for their "Snowed In" special and again during MTV's "Spring Break 2000."

Beauty Q&A

Like any girl on the planet, Mandy has her bad hair days and skin breakouts, but she's learned how to handle beauty emergencies. Here are some common hair and make-up questions that even pop stars ask.

How do I keep my lips from being chapped?

Kick your lip-licking habit, remove any dead skin with a dry toothbrush, and apply lots of gloss, like Mandy does. Her fave lip gloss is cotton candy or strawberry.

My foundation looks caked on. How can I get glowing skin? Mandy drinks gallons of water which keeps skin healthy. She mixes her moisturizer with her foundation so it's thinner in texture and therefore lighter on the skin. She also likes to enhance her cheekbones with dustings of shimmery powder.

When I wear mascara, it smudges so I end up with raccoon eyes, even if it's waterproof mascara. Is there an alternative? Mandy likes clear mascara for the very reason that she doesn't want black circles under her eyes. Clear mascara is handy if you're sweating a lot from exercising or in Mandy's case, performing on stage.

What's a good tip for ultra-shiny lips? Mandy has tried MAC's Lip Glass and was very happy with the result. It literally makes your lips shine like they're made out of glass.

How can I bring out my eyes? Mandy doesn't like to overdo her eye make-up, so she sweeps shimmery, pastel eye shadow on her lids for big, beautiful eyes.

How can I get super-straight hair? Mandy protects, nourishes and softens her locks with a deep conditioner. She likes to use hair products from Redken. She gets her hair stick-straight with a flattening iron.

I get frustrated with flyaways – or baby hairs as I call them. How can I smooth them down? When Mandy wants to flatten flyaways she has said that a good tip is to spritz hairspray on an old toothbrush and brush it through the unruly strands.

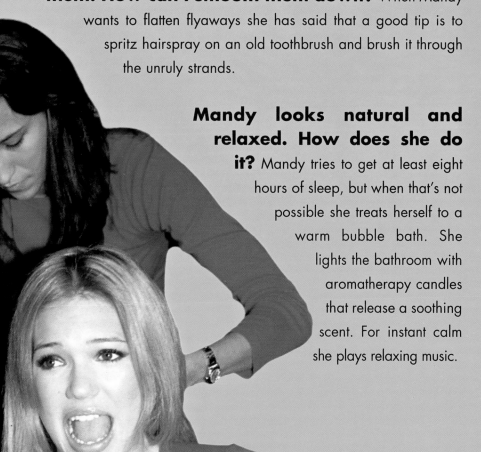

Mandy looks natural and relaxed. How does she do it? Mandy tries to get at least eight hours of sleep, but when that's not possible she treats herself to a warm bubble bath. She lights the bathroom with aromatherapy candles that release a soothing scent. For instant calm she plays relaxing music.

How can I jazz up my hair without doing anything drastic? A stylist sprinkled glitter into hair gel and slicked it on Mandy's hair for a cool new look, so now Mandy does it herself using blue or silver glitter. To update a simple style, Mandy creates a zigzag parting and accessorizes her hair with Velcro-backed hair jewels or sparkly mini clips. She also uses texturizing gels from Fudge hair products and she visits beauty websites to learn about new products.

When I'm stressed you can see it on my face. How do I wipe out the worry look? When Mandy is feeling tense, she treats herself to a massage. Recruit a friend or sibling to give you a neck rub. Promise them one in return and they'll most likely agree to it.

Shopping With Mandy

Chapter Six

ONE OF THE PERKS OF BEING A PERFORMER IS THAT YOU get to wear a variety of cool clothes, whether it's an industrial flight suit that glows in the dark for an evening concert, or a light pink organza sundress for an awards show. Mandy has always had a passion for fashion, and she remembers dressing up as a kid and walking around the house in her mother's high heels. Growing up, little Mandy took a liking to Madonna's 1980s look, so she wore everything from ripped jeans and biker shorts to fluorescent bandannas. She has said that there are still photos kicking around the house to remind her of those childhood days. Although a lot has changed for Mandy – for instance, she's moved on from the ripped jeans look – one thing that has stayed the same is her love for fun and stylish outfits. She could shop till she drops, but her busy schedule doesn't allow her much time for spending sprees. This can be a tease

because the different countries she travels to offer completely different clothes that she wouldn't be able to find in America. Mandy was in London when she celebrated her sixteenth birthday on April 10, 2000, and for once she did have the chance to check out the shops in one of the most fashionable cities in the world.

If you managed to get Mandy away from the recording studio or tour bus for a few hours to go shopping, you would have a blast because Mandy has an appetite for awesome attire that makes even the biggest shopper look like an amateur. Your shopping marathon would probably take place in a mall because Mandy likes stores where she can find cool clothes without high-end designer price tags. You'd probably make your first stop at Guess, where Mandy had picked up a pink top and vibrant floor-length skirt for the *Billboard* Music

Awards. Then you'd swing by Wet Seal and Contempo Casuals – Mandy modelled for them, after all – for some trendy getups. She likes to look for bright tops – orange or hot pink – and she usually wears solids instead of patterns.

In the song "Summer Girls" the group LFO sings about the girl who wears Abercrombie & Fitch. LFO must have been talking about Mandy because she loves A&F's comfy and casual clothes. After picking up some khakis and cotton shirts, you and Mandy would probably check out the jeans at Diesel or the leather pants at Tommy Hilfiger. In fact, Mandy modelled for Tommy Hilfiger at his "Young, Loud & Sexy" fashion show this winter in New York. She joined artists like Mary J. Blige on the runway wearing a pink camouflage top and leather pants.

When she graced the cover of *Teen People* for their "25 Hottest Stars Under 25" issue, Mandy wore a white sequined top on the cover and a pink sequined dress for the inside article. She's performed in expressive tops with words like "Rock Star" scrawled on the front in diamond studs, and she likes to apply temporary crystal tattoos on her forearm for fun. She's worn everything from fringed pants and feathered halter tops to jean skirts and sandals, but the outfit Mandy likes best of all is a pair of worn jeans and a relaxed T-shirt. She has said that you don't need fancy clothes to look and feel beautiful.

Mandy also knows that fashion emergencies can happen any time, so don't worry if you get a run in your stocking, or your pants split by accident. Mandy's had her fair share of disasters, and remembers the time she was out with her friends when the heel of her shoe broke and she had to go shoeless all night.

Chapter Seven

Bonding With Her Best Buds

LIFE ON TOUR CAN BE LONELY FOR PERFORMERS BECAUSE THEY'RE AWAY from their family and friends. Mandy luckily has extra support because she always travels with a parent, whether it's her mother Stacy or her father Don, who is an airline pilot and can arrange his schedule to coincide with Mandy's worldwide stops. Sometimes Mandy brings her brothers along if they don't have school, and if she had her way she would invite all of her friends to join her on tour too. That's not always possible, so Mandy relies heavily on the phone and e-mail to keep in touch with her long-distance pals. She has said that it's tough to be away from her friends and she misses spending quality time with the girls watching videos, snacking on the couch and giving each other beauty makeovers. She knows that there's a trade-off and you have to sacrifice some things to become a successful pop star.

Mandy has said that when she first started recording it put a strain on her friendships, because she was devoting her time to the studio and not her friends. They are incredibly important to her, so once she explained that she was pursuing her dreams but would make any effort possible to hang out with them, her friends understood and have supported her ever since.

This faithful friend tries to squeeze in time with her pals whenever possible, and had the chance to bond with her best bud Bonnie when she appeared as an extra in Mandy's video "Walk Me Home." Mandy had a great time bringing her friends to the premiere of *Center Stage* to hear the debut of her song "I Wanna Be With You." She has said that she gets both nervous and excited when she's performing in her hometown of Orlando because she knows that her friends and classmates are watching her in the audience.

When it comes to friendship, Mandy has said that she looks for a pal who is like her – sensitive and honest – and supports her in the crazy pop world that she's plunged into. Even though she radiates self-confidence when she's performing on stage, promoting Neutrogena or hosting a show on MTV, Mandy admits she's secretly quite shy when she first meets someone. When she truly gets to know someone and builds a trust, Mandy is a loyal friend to the end.

With Mandy's ever increasing involvement with MTV, she's had the chance to develop friendships with VJ's Carson Daly, Brian McFayden, Ananda Lewis and the rest of the crew. She's also close to her dancers, so when one of them discovered that his cell phone was stolen, Mandy stepped in like only a true pal would. She called up the number and yelled at the guy who had bought the stolen cell phone off the street.

Mandy's new-found fans are also her friends, and she often rushes to her laptop whenever she has a spare minute to e-mail a letter to them on her website. She's also very willing to laugh at herself — she recently wrote an e-mail to her fans saying "thanks for putting up with the dork in me."

Chapter Eight

BET YOU DIDN'T KNOW THAT MANDY HAD A CERTAIN BOY ON THE brain while recording "Candy" – specifically an ex-boyfriend – something she has said actually helped her bring an honesty or "grit" to her performance. In fact, Mandy insists on drawing from real life issues to bring meaning to all her music and she refuses to sing about something she's never experienced. While working on "Candy" in the studio, Mandy let herself think about a former crush who she still liked but was mad at, and that helped bring the song to life. This special sweetie was one of her first serious boyfriends, and they dated for about three months, going to the movies and dinner instead of just casually hanging out after school.

Stepping into the spotlight means being surrounded by gossip and Mandy is no stranger to tabloid fodder. She has been falsely linked with a number of other stars. One of the biggest myths is that Mandy is dating Backstreet Boy Nick Carter. She has said that he's "a great guy" but he's 20 and too old. When she told Nick about the story he laughed with surprise. False reports have also linked her with pop cutie Taylor Hanson, as well as Carson Daly and Brian McFayden from MTV. While they're all sweet guys, Mandy doesn't like the tabloids "fixing her up." Mandy does admit she's a sucker for English and Irish accents, and is crazy about the group Westlife. She also admits to fancying actor Ryan Phillippe, although he's now married to actress Reese Witherspoon and has a baby girl so he's off limits.

Currently Mandy does not have a boyfriend, although she's keeping her eyes peeled for the perfect guy. The boys reading this book might be interested to

learn that the songster is pretty picky. Mandy is model tall so she looks for a guy who is even taller – at least six feet – and who can dance with her even if she's wearing high heels. She doesn't like flashy guys who care too much about impressing others, but she admits she melts when a guy splashes on Dolce & Gabbana cologne. Mandy doesn't like guys who smoke because cigarettes give you stinky breath and she's allergic to the smoke – it puffs up her eyes and closes up her throat, she has said.

Mandy lives by the golden rule that what comes around goes around, so she looks for an honest guy who doesn't play games. She wants her future boyfriend to be sensitive, talkative, spontaneous, supportive and funny – Mandy refuses to settle for second best. She would have no problem asking a guy out because she thinks some guys are just too shy to make the first move. She has said that if she really liked a guy and wanted to get him to notice her, she would try to find out about him first to see if they have common interests and then strike up a conversation. Mandy is an Aries so

Mandy does admit she's a sucker for English and Irish accents, and is crazy about the group Westlife.

she's playful, strong-willed and direct – this bold beauty has no problem looking a guy in the eye – so she needs to meet her match and find a guy who won't duck for cover if she happens to glance in his direction. Mandy has said that looks aren't terribly important and she is much more focused on a friendly personality.

You would assume Mandy gets asked out a lot, but her schedule is so jam-packed that there's little time to meet a guy let alone talk to one for a few minutes. She has said that it's weird when guy fans compliment her because she wasn't popular in school. She admits she wasn't one of the girls who got the guys in school. During autograph sessions, Mandy has said that the girls have no problem coming up to her and talking, but that the guys stand back and watch her shyly with their friends.

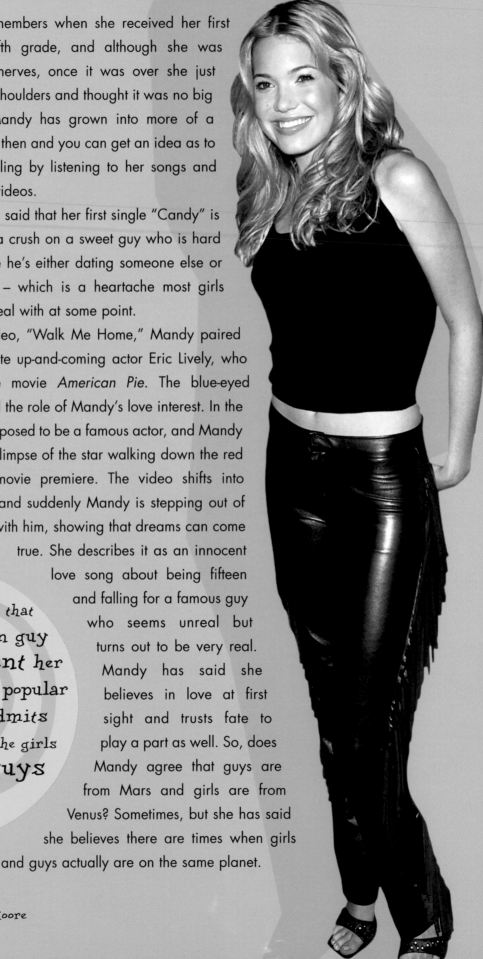

Mandy remembers when she received her first kiss in the fifth grade, and although she was shaking with nerves, once it was over she just shrugged her shoulders and thought it was no big deal. Well, Mandy has grown into more of a romantic since then and you can get an idea as to what she's feeling by listening to her songs and watching her videos.

Mandy has said that her first single "Candy" is about having a crush on a sweet guy who is hard to get because he's either dating someone else or moving away – which is a heartache most girls have had to deal with at some point.

For her video, "Walk Me Home," Mandy paired up with the cute up-and-coming actor Eric Lively, who starred in the movie *American Pie*. The blue-eyed sweetie played the role of Mandy's love interest. In the video he is supposed to be a famous actor, and Mandy tries to get a glimpse of the star walking down the red carpet at a movie premiere. The video shifts into fantasy mode and suddenly Mandy is stepping out of the limousine with him, showing that dreams can come true. She describes it as an innocent love song about being fifteen and falling for a famous guy who seems unreal but turns out to be very real.

She has said that it's weird when guy fans compliment her because she wasn't popular in school. She admits she wasn't one of the girls who got the guys in school

Mandy has said she believes in love at first sight and trusts fate to play a part as well. So, does Mandy agree that guys are from Mars and girls are from Venus? Sometimes, but she has said she believes there are times when girls and guys actually are on the same planet.

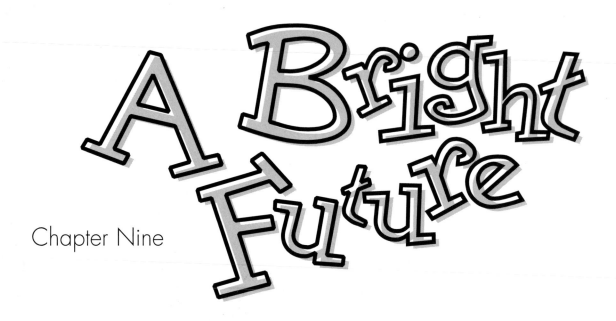

A Bright Future

Chapter Nine

INDUSTRY INSIDERS PREDICT A LASTING CAREER FOR MANDY AND SEE HER continuing her talents in music, television, and even movies. Mandy is currently looking at scripts for feature films and there's a chance fans will be able to see her on the big screen. Her producers have said that they believe Mandy's popularity is based on her warm voice and her sweet personality. She doesn't have an overly booming voice like a diva, but she doesn't have the overly inflated ego of one either. According to her producers she's a "good" kid – she's down-to-earth, close to her family and grounded in the real world. That rare combination is vital for an artist's personal growth and commercial appeal. Recently, more than fifteen million votes were counted for Nickelodeon's 13th Annual Kids' Choice Awards, and the winner of "Favorite Rising Star" was none other than Mandy.

Mandy has just scratched the surface of her career. In the next year she will be writing more lyrics and melodies, practising the guitar and getting involved in producing. Aside from fulfilling her duties as the new Neutrogena girl, Mandy is studying hard to maintain straight As and is fluent in French. She would like to attend New York University and study journalism – Mandy loves to write essays, poems and short stories.

This multi-talented and versatile star would like to follow in the footsteps of her inspirations, Madonna and Bette Midler, who continue to devote themselves to new projects and grow as artists. Mandy still remembers that rush from watching *Oklahoma* when she was a kid, and in her heart she hopes to one day perform in a rock musical on Broadway. During a live internet chat she said, "My main goals are to be happy, have fun and stay healthy. Whatever the future holds, with family and friends, I'm set."

Quiz:

How Well Do You Know Mandy?

1. What size shoe does Mandy wear?
A. 8
B. 9
C. 10

2. What is Mandy's least fave subject?
A. English
B. Mathematics
C. French

3. What does Mandy drink before she performs?
A. Milk
B. Orange juice
C. Hot water with a twist of orange

4. If she wasn't performing, Mandy would like to try a career in:
A. Education
B. Journalism
C. Law

5. What sport did Mandy enjoy playing in school?

A. Lacrosse

B. Basketball

C. Archery

6. When Mandy auditioned for Sony, what kind of song did she sing?

A. A pop song

B. An R&B ballad

C. A Broadway show tune

7. Which group did Mandy first tour with?

A. Backstreet Boys

B. 'N Sync

C. Limp Bizkit

8. Mandy has a beauty contract with

A. Cover Girl

B. Chanel

C. Neutrogena

9. What are the names of Mandy's three cats?

A. Zoe, Otis, Fritz

B. Milo, Chloe, Zoe

C. Pepper, Milo, Garfield

10. Mandy can't live without:

A. Her cell phone

B. Lip gloss

C. Cotton candy

ANSWERS: 1. Answer: C 2. Answer: B 3. Answer: B 4. Answer: C 5. Answer: A 6. Answer: C 7. Answer: B 8. Answer: C 9. Answer: B 10. Answer: All three

Discography

Singles
"Candy"
Sony 550/Epic, Released August 17, 1999

Albums
So Real
Sony 550/Epic, Released Dec 7, 1999

So Real/Candy/What You Want/Walk Me Home/Lock Me In Your Heart/Telephone (interlude)/Quit Breaking My Heart/Let Me Be The One/Not Too Young/Love Shot/I Like It/Love You For Always/Quit Breaking My Heart (reprise)

I Wanna Be With You
Sony 550/Epic, Released May 9, 2000

I Wanna Be With You/Everything My Heart Desires/Want You Back/Way To My Heart/So Real (Wade Robson Remix)/Lock Me In Your Heart/Walk Me Home/I Like It/So Real/Candy (Wade Robson Remix)/Your Face/I Wanna Be With You (Soul Solution Remix)

Soundtracks
Center Stage
Sony/Epic, Released April 18, 2000

I Wanna Be With You – Mandy Moore/First Kiss – International Five/Don't Get Lost In The Crowd – Ashley Ballard/We're Dancing – P.Y.T./Friends Forever – Thunderbugs/Get Used To This – Cyrena/A Girl Can Dream – P.Y.T./Cosmic Girl – Jamiroquai/Higher Ground – Red Hot Chili Peppers/Come Baby Come – Elvis Crespo and Gizelle D'Cole/The Way You Make Me Feel – Michael Jackson/If I Was The One – Riff Endz/Canned Heat – Jamiroquai/
I Wanna Be With You (Soul Solution Remix) – Mandy Moore